monographs on the ancient near east

volume 1, fascicle 4

the conceptual autonomy of the babylonian world

by

benno landsberger

translation by t. jacobsen, b. foster, h. von siebenthal

introduction by t. jacobsen

undena publications

malibu 1976

BENNO LANDSBERGER
(1890-1968)

Benno Landsberger died in Chicago on the twenty-sixth of April, 1968, after a short illness. One of the greatest Assyriologists of all time, he was elected a member of the American Pilosophical Society in 1959.

Landsberger was born April 21, 1890, in Friedeck in what was then Austrian Silesia. After finishing Gymnasium in Friedeck he attended the University of Leipzig, where he studied under Heinrich Zimmern and the Arabist August Fischer. He obtained his doctor's degree in 1914 and published an enlarged form of his thesis in 1915. It was the still unsurpassed study,
[141] *Der Kultische Kalender der Babylonier und Assyrer.* In World War I, Landsberger served
in the Austrian army on the eastern front. After the war he returned to Leipzig to teach. He became professor extraordinary in 1926, was called to the University of Marburg in 1928 as successor to Peter Jensen, but returned to Leipzig in 1929 to succeed his teacher Zimmern who was retiring. The years in Leipzig were fruitful and productive years for Landsberger, who soon gathered around him a remarkable group of talented pupils. In 1935, however, he was dismissed from his position by the National Socialist Government of Germany and moved to Ankara in Turkey, where he had accepted a professorship at the University of Ankara. In 1948, finally, he was called to Chicago as professor in the Oriental Institute of the University of Chicago. Here he taught until his retirement in 1955, but continued afterwards his research and work on the Assyrian Dictionary. His mind was clear and penetrating to the last, and one important article after the other flowed from his pen in a steady stream till very shortly before his death.

Landsberger was the acknowledged master in the field of Assyriology, unrivaled in knowledge and competence. Before all else, perhaps, he was the philologist, and as philologist specifically the lexicographer. His incredible memory laid to hand any and every text he had ever read, and he had read practically all of cuneiform literature. To this came the keenest insight and the highest standards of precision. He was a poet seeking the *mot juste* and rejecting anything less. His patience and perseverance when he was on the track of an elusive meaning were wonderful to watch. Guided by what he called "Fingerspitzengefuhl" he would gradually move closer to what the word could mean, constantly dissatisfied with approximations, critically aware of distance from the vaguely sensed truth, until at last--sometimes, but by no means always--there would come the moment of "Zugreifen." The clear, uncompromising, pregnantly concrete rendering was found.

Landsberger's forte was the concrete. He had an artist's sensitivity and ability to project himself into an ancient context and to sense what would have been said or felt or indicated, what the unknown word had to convey. Abstract structure held little appeal for him. He was himself aware of the fact that his particular genius did not run to the writing of books, but to articles;
[142] and even in his articles the joy and the enlightenment are likely to come from a succession
of brilliant specific insights rather than from the overarching problem and structuring of the investigation. It is characteristic that he won his spurs in a series of reviews for which the structure was in a sense given with the book under review, but which so brilliantly and decisively advanced the book's subject as almost to dwarf it. The Assyrian dialect was lucidly analyzed and presented in two reviews of books by Julius Lewy; a review of Ungnad's *Babylonische Briefe* signally improved upon a book which in itself was a masterpiece; the review of Gadd and Legrain, *Ur Excavations Text I,* did more to elucidate the texts and their historical context than long books could have done.

Landsberger's ability to project himself sensitively into a given situation governed by forms and values of a culture so removed in time and place from ours as is ancient Mesopotamian culture was at the core of his rebellion against the state of Assyriology as he found it--as handmaiden to Old Testament studies, determined in setting and solving of problems by the one aim of throwing light on Old Testament data. Landsberger's programmatic article of 1926, "Die Eigenbegrifflichkeit der Babylonischen Welt" (*Islamica* 2: pp. 355-372) insisted on the necessity of studying Mesopotamian culture for its own sake, in its own terms, and within its own system of values. Under the banner of "Eigenbegrifflichkeit" Landsberger and his students may be said to have made Assyriology for the first time an autonomous discipline. [This is the article translated in the present fascicle.]

Central in Landsberger's interest was in those years Akkadian grammar, which he analyzed with power and imagination. Fortunately, most of his results have now been made available by his pupil von Soden in the latter's great *Grundriss der Akkadischen Grammatik.* For many years, surviving in private lecture notes circulating among scholars, they constituted an exciting, but tantalizing, secret lore only.

Landsberger's concern with "Eigenbegrifflichkeit" might of itself have led him to the Ancients' own study of words and ideas and their organization of their insights in the ancient lexical texts. As it happened, however, it was an invitation from the Chicago Assyrian Dictionary to prepare these texts for use in the dictionary work that firmly set his foot on the path that was to open up a whole new dimension of cuneiform studies. The incredibly knowledgeable, systematic,
[143] and methodical study which through the years he devoted to the identification of individual lexical series, to the principles governing ancient lexicography, to the ferreting out of the meanings of new and obscure words, staggers the imagination. I wonder whether it would be an exaggeration to say that close to half of our knowledge of Akkadian at present is significantly modified by, or wholly due to, his contributions.

In attempting to gauge what Landsberger has done for the field of Assyriology one may not, however, lose oneself entirely in what he has done directly to the exclusion of what he has contributed in more subtle ways. An elite of Assyriologists today are his pupils; but in a broader sense all Assyriologists deserving of the name are his pupils, have been influenced and molded by the fervor of his commitment to the field, by the challenge of his almost unattainable standards of excellence in terms of knowledge and judgment, and by the amusing, human, unconventional, scholarly arrogant, challenging--and, of course, often deplorable--anecdotes that circulated about him--a surprising number of them true. Perhaps nothing else measures as fully the loss we have suffered as this: that no present personality in the field is genuine enough, controversial enough, and striking enough to be worth telling anecdotes about. His death leaves Assyriologists, as scholars and as men impoverished.

1970 Thorkild Jacobsen

Editors' Note. - The introduction above is reprinted from the *Year Book of the American Philosophical Society,* 1970, pp. 140-143.

The article by Landsberger which follows is a translation of "Die Eigenbegrifflichkeit der Babylonischen Welt." *Islamica* 2 (1926) 355-72 (reprint Darmstadt 1965). The translation is the result of a joint effort of the three individuals named on the title page: two separate translations of the German text were independently made available to the editors by B. Foster from Yale and H. von Siebenthal from the University of Liverpool; the present version was then prepared by Th. Jacobsen on the basis of those two versions and, of course, the original text. Numbers in square brackets in the left-hand margin refer to the beginning of a new page in the original editions.

The Conceptual Autonomy of the Babylonian World

A Lecture by Benno Landsberger

At the beginning of the last century determined inquirers gained access to Babylonian Antiquity along the narrow pathway of a most scant tradition. That, however, was a far cry from actually reawakening to life that ancient civilization. The prospects of that distant dream being realized improved significantly only in 1847 with the lucky find of the most complete library in which the canon of Babylonian literature had ever been collected. When in 1872 a tablet from this library yielded up its general sense to the decipherers, it proved to contain the story of the Flood, whose primitive form aroused tremendous interest throughout the whole world in the new scientific adventure. No matter what motives aroused this interest amongst the general public, governments, and patrons of science, the following eighty years' excavations, only occasionally interrupted, have filled the museums with such a flood of written material, both literary documents and political and economic ones, that even a first sifting of all the material coming, as it does, from a span of three millennia, proves quite impossible for the handful of workers available. The continuing influx of urgent tasks has hardly ever allowed Assyriology leisure to reflect upon itself and to reach an awareness of where it was heading. Today may, therefore, well be the first time that an attempt is made to bring nearer to its solution the problem: To what extent is it possible to reconstruct
[356] *vividly* and *faithfully* an ancient, alien civilization by philological means, without the help of a tradition continuing down to the present day? Granted, even Assyriology is not without some tradition: The pioneers of our science could at least start from the linguistic relationship with the other Semitic languages and from the numerous words borrowed from Assyro-Babylonian by the language of the Aramaeans, who took over the material culture of the former. This was a great help, but at the same time a dangerous source of error, which the present generation is still struggling to eliminate. Misinterpretations caused by mechanical adoption of traditional opinion are deeply rooted. An example may serve as illustration: in every (Akkadian) sentence there are forms with a *t* infix; up to this day they have generally been regarded as reflexive, because similar forms in the other Semitic languages have always been explained as reflexives, in spite of the fact that this designation is only valid for Arabic, rarely for Hebrew and Aramic, and never at any rate for Assyro-Bablonian.

In general, however, the spirit of reconstruction had free sway. In their enthusiasm of discovery the early decipherers often imbued the simple monuments with far too much of their own ideas and so gave Assyriology a reputation for fancifulness.

FRIEDRICH DELITZSCH imposed on this freely creative fantasy the fetters of sound methodology and laid the foundations of our philology by quiet, persevering work, uninfluenced by sensationalism. Building upon these foundations HEINRICH ZIMMERN with his refined sense of form was able in empathy with Babylonian lyric poetry to make it enjoyable to us as poetry - though only as far as the best pieces are concerned. PETER JENSEN, on the other hand, with his firm grasp and sure realistic aim reproduced and effectively communicated elemental epic power, for instance in his renderings of the fragments which tell us of life-seeking Gilgamesh.

However, these works which seem to us achievements of the highest order proving the indestructability of works of art, are but small islands in the ocean of materials that mean nothing to us when naively viewed. The scholarship of the Babylonians seems abstruse to us, their religion in most of its forms barren superstition, their legal system primitive. Thus the scholar faces his own subject unmoved and aloof, and precisely those men to whom our science owes most look for more rewarding research problems outside their field. They are trying - and this was the impulse [357] which brought Assyriology into existence - to make dead things alive by connecting them up with ideas that are still of importance to us or to civilizations close to us. The approach of 'the history of ideas' attempts to find so-called "cultural elements," which can be regarded in a manner of speaking as the germ-cells of the later, more complex structures. This approach, aiming at establishing a living tradition of civilization reaching back to earliest times, is but one special representative of the general evolutionist approach. That, too, deals with the so-called more primitive civilizations as preparatory stages for higher ones, partly in order to make it possible to see the course of world history as one, partly also to provide living models of primitive conditions for the historians of civilization who use genetic explanations and so necessarily must seek to reconstruct primitive conditions. Valuable and rewarding as these approaches may be, it goes without saying that they are justifiable only *a posteriori* when applied to well-explored matter. As a principle of research applied from the outset, however, they must inevitably narrow our perspective in advance, and they axiomatically presuppose - in spite of its vagueness - the concept of evolution, which ought in fact to find clarification only as a result of our work. In the approach that I have tried to adopt - I should like to designate it as the *general approach of the humanities* - I too have endeavoured to keep Babylonian civilization in a living relation with the other branches of the history of civilization as do the two schools mentioned above. But there is a difference: this living connection is not derived from historical contacts or origins, that is to say, not from the fact that the Babylonians along with the Egyptians were our spiritual fathers, or that they represent a type of the so-called semi-culture (*Halbkultur*), a stage through which mankind had to pass, the inter-connection that I have in mind is given with the unity of the object of study, the human mind, and becomes self-evident as we try to find our way into the depths of the Babylonian conceptual world. All understanding consists first of all in establishing some link between the alien world and our own. In the initial stage this is expressed by a number of simple equations, which are compiled in grammar and lexicon, *e.g.* ending *-um* nominative singular, root *halak* "to go"; but such full equations are possible only to a limited extent, most often we have to content ourselves with partial equations of the type: part of the Babylonian concept *x* corresponds with part of our concept *y*. All these [358] equations are correct in so far as both *a* and *b* are beyond any doubt.

However, this is, so to speak, only the simple algebra of comprehension. A grammar or lexicon thus organized does not tell us the slightest thing about the characteristics of the Babylonian mind. Also a combination of these concepts, therefore, can never result in a faithful portrayal of life, even though an historian who is trained by the analogy of other peoples may set up a structure out of such elements, and even if the intuition of a philologist may reproduce from them a work of art. Rather, if we are not to deprive ourselves of the most important key to understanding we seek out the conceptual autonomy of a *particular* civilization, and it is to this task that my own work has been devoted for the last few years, some results of which I am here presenting in brief.

The method used has been *heuristic*, that is to say, it does not approach the alien mind from a *fixed* system of *conceptual referents* in order to find out to what extent this alien civilization can be related to it. Were I to proceed in that way I could always only find again in my object what I already had within my own perspective. Rather, the standard applicable to the world of ideas to be unravelled must be derived from it itself. Finding the conceptual currency standard for a civilization comes about in the manner that what is being related, and what it is being related to, mutually move closer to each other, both attaining to greater clarity and distinctiveness.

But the scholar needs to have at his disposal a full and rich system of the possible concepts of life, and this cannot be derived from his constructive imagination, nor are the types sufficient which the comparative study of civilization provides—e.g. neither imperfective in language, nor polytheism in religion, nor marriage by purchase in the legal system and so forth. What is required is a familiarity with the nature of language as language, of religion as religion, of law as law. The individual scholar, however, cannot possibly have such a wide experience. He must get in touch with people who have studied these disciplines as they relate to other peoples and, where possible, to living ones; such viable exchange is vital for the application of this method. The philologist's poverty of abstract concepts always has for counterpart the generalist's lack of tangible particulars. To strike the proper balance and so attain to rich and fully developed
[359] concepts of life is the common aim of both the specialist and the generalist scholar. Neither the narrowly conceived adjustments of the philologist who does not look beyond the pale of his own field, nor the shallow typologies of the comparative historian of civilization, who thinks he can make do with one abstract, formal pattern for all the various objectivizations of the human mind, can be allowed to prevail.

The autonomous concepts thus obtained now have to be connected into *systems*, the first of which is the system of autonomous grammatical concepts, which will immediately lead us on to the concept of the so-called "inner form" of language. This may be followed by the system of concepts relating to the apprehension of space, then as we move on and on to more specific features we may finally reach the closed systems of certain special disciplines or professions as for instance those of law and commerce. Only by way of constructing the system of concepts can we find our way into the nature of a civilization. Without this higher mathematics of the autonomous concepts, from mere ordinary algebra as I have presented it, only disjointed compilation can arise, not true intellectual unity.

Now if the method just outlined in very abstract fashion is to be illustrated with the example of grammar, from where we have to start anyway, our basic principle must be not to apply to the Akkadian language (this is the term for the language of Mesopotamia as represented by the Babylonian and Assyrian dialects) a standard derived from current grammar, rather, we must derive it from Akkadian itself heuristically. It is not only that it would be impossible to cope with the wide spectrum of verbal themes in Akkadian by means of ordinary categories such as present, preterite, etc., but even seemingly obvious categories such as verb, noun, third person, accusative have a special force in Akkadian which not only differs from those in languages familiar to us, but also from those in other Semitic languages, so that they have to be defined accordingly. Three themes run, as with the South-Arabic-Ethiopic verb, through the Akkadian verb as well. It is governed by the dualism between *momentary* or *punctual* on the one hand, and durative on the other. The momentary aspect has one theme (*i-kšud*), the durative two (*kašid* and *i-kašad*). The latter however, are identical in form and nature. The only difference between them resides in the fact that the first one expresses a state, the second one a durative occur-
[360] rence. Occurrences are marked by the prefixing of the pronominal elements, states by affixing them. This distinction of state and occurrence is also characteristic of the Hebrew verb, but Akkadian differs from Hebrew in so far as this distinction in Akkadian is not combined with the distinction between the analytical and the synthetical sentence. Hebrew uses one form of sentence when a concept that has been perceived is merely being analyzed into its elements and a different form when the object of perception is being vividly rebuilt, whether, so to speak, the picture of a state or an occurrence is being *examined* or *painted*; subjects and predicates differ in their position towards one another, the latter also with respect to verbal theme, the so-called tense. States here belong to the analytical theme, occurrences, however, to either type according to the aspect of the speaker, *i.e.* according to whether he analyzed the concept

or builds it up again. Akkadian on the other hand only knows the analytical type and even the so-called tense is independent of the aspect[1] of the speaker. That aspect was current in prehistoric periods can be deduced from the difference between the prefixing and the affixing conjugations. The Akkadian handed down to us, however, has that rigid character, compared to the labile, flowing character of Hebrew, which is a main feature of this language as a whole. From this follows further the factor of the *objectivity* of the statement, that is to say the occurrence or state is viewed as such, independently of the standpoint of the speaker. The specific character of Akkadian however is constituted by the differentiations within the concept of process or of state on the basis of a very rich spectrum of themes. As we have seen with every verb, we must differentiate in the first place between the punctual and the durative with its subcategories of stative and of fientic durative. The stative does not distinguish between a predicative statement, "he sleeps" or an attributive one, "he is red."

The fientic durative by nature is always predicative, but it becomes attributive by simply drop-
[361] ping the pronominal prefix, *isarriq* "he squints" in the sense of "he looks frequently askance at," on the other hand *sarriq* "he squints" in the sense of "he is cross-eyed."[2] In the fully developed Akkadian system the punctual at one and the same time denotes the starting point of a durative action, that is to say it functions as an ingressive or a terminative; with verbs of motion the terminative is marked as such by the so-called ventive, *i.e.* by an ending (*-am*) which originally denoted direction towards the speaker. The durative does not distinguish subjective time phases: *irappud* means "he ran," "he runs," "he will run." That was originally the case with the punctual as well, but here differentiation of the three stages of subjective time has been achieved secondarily by the following means: a punctual present is, just as in Slavonic, which is closest to Akkadian as far as the system of aspects (Aktionsarten) is concerned, a *contradictio in adiecto*). The present as such expresses the idea of being engaged in doing something and is therefore a durative, and the punctual present is formed as in Slavonic by substituting the iterative form for it. In Akkadian, however, this form is made up by the addition of a *t*-infix, which is not parallelled in any other Semitic language but is so in the North African group of Hamitic languages.[3] Whatever little Akkadian distinguishes in the way of modes is likewise expressed with the aid of the aspects (*Aktionsarten*): every durative is by nature indicative, the imperative, on the other hand, is by nature punctual, that is to say I can only express "start moving!", but not at the same time "go strolling for an hour!".

But to the very spirit of the Akkadian language we penetrate only with the fundamental observation that the verbal themes (in the cases both of the triconsonantal and especially of the

---

1. Differing from Indo-European usage I try to introduce the term *aspect* in contradistinction to the objective *'Aktionsart'* for the varying use of the 'tenses' according to the attitude of the speaker (for example experience, report, simple statement etc.).

2. This is a favorably chosen example; similarly *iḫabbat: ḫabbat* (to rob); sometimes however the final vowel changes.

3. The punctual present is a formational compromise inasmuch as the iterative, if used as a punctual present, is stressed on the first syllable in the manner of the punctuals, *ittallak* "he goes, went (all the time)", *ittalak* "he is going (away, now)".

biconsonantal verb) represent each a class of *meaning* —in the case of triconsonantal verbs the meaning is linked with the variable vowel between the second and the third radical, in the case
[362] of biconsonantal verbs it is linked with the particular pattern of each theme, *e.g. kūn, dīn, damum* (doubling of the second consonant), *lid* with optional augment *wa*. In order to find our way to these classes of meaning, we must add to the pairs of categories already recognized, punctual:durative and fientive:stative, yet the following: the fientives are voluntative or involuntative, that is to say, evoked by the will of the subject of the sentence or not. If involuntative, we have to distinguish two sub-categories, the automative and the passive proper, *i.e.* that which happens to the subject automatically and that which affects the subject due to external causes. What happens can be characterized as an act of the subject or as an occurrence with respect to the object, *e.g.* "to write," but "to whitewash a wall" (subject or object orientation, only in the latter case is the passive possible, the object of the act becoming the subject of the sentence); the occurrence may be terminate or non-terminate, that is to say there is or there is not a natural end point, *e.g.* "to write," but "to knead a batch of dough" or "to hunt a piece of game"; moreover there are differences in the way an act is being done: chain or linear durative, *e.g.* "to thread pearls," but "to turn a wheel"; differences in the way an occurrence takes place (subitative, successive, inchoative); further the event may be resultative or not, *e.g.* if I fetch a loaf of bread from the baker, the loaf will not be regarded subsequently as "fetched", but a broken object remains broken; or, again the result is a so-called outcome (*Erscheinung*), *e.g.* a judiciary sentence is by nature the result of judging. In this way we have arrived at a table of the categories of Akkadian perception, which we can use as a standard as we seek to ascertain the classes of meaning of the verb. However, not all categories are distinguished with every theme, *e.g.* the theme *rapud* "to run" is already determined by the categories fientive, durative, and intransitive, and in return is indifferent with regard to voluntative, subject-orientedness and resultative. On the other hand this table is still insufficient if all the nuances are to be subsumed by our system, for instance the themes *mūt* "to die", *nūḫ* "to come to rest", or its converse *nūš* "to start moving," belong to a class which denotes the sudden transition from a normal state of existence into the opposite one. Their transitive correspondences are found in the class of terminate duratives, *e.g. ṣūd* "to hunt a piece of game", *dūk* "to kill." These complicated classes of occurrences which bring to our minds how immensely rich this language is in expressiveness is not by any means peculiar to Akkadian, it belongs to all the Semitic languages, at least as far as the biconsonantal verb is
[363] concerned, and particularly to Hebrew and Aramaic. Arabic on the other hand went its own way during the period when it acquired its wealth of roots greater than that of any other Semitic language. If my results prove to be correct they are of a significance for the history of human development not to be underrated; for with their help we shall be able to reconstruct with certainty the concept of occurrence, intricate as it is and refined in structure, for the time before the Semitic languages divided, *i.e.* for the period of earliest history which is beyond our chronological reckoning; we would thus move closer to language beginnings than will ever be possible with the Indo-European languages. We also get this impression of a structure that is logically differentiated and thought through when we analyze the structure of the language as a whole (here again speaking of Akkadian, although much is equally true of Semitic in general.) It is not the outward difference between conjugability and declinability that constitutes the essential difference between verb and substantive, rather only the pure noun (*Substantive*), the genuine concept of an object is a substantive (*Nomen*) in the true sense. To the early Semite, however, only the bearer of invariable, lasting characteristics is an object *e.g.* names of materials, of animals, of members of the body. Logically these are clearly kept apart from the so-called outcomes (*Erscheinungen*), thus snow *e.g.* is an object, because it is an independent bearer of characteristics, rain on the other hand and light are manifestations - they do not belong to the noun, but to the verb, they are all formed as the results of processes. In the same way all adjectives belong to the verb; the adjective is merely a variety of the durative. In this case

too, marking it off from the noun is not superficial in character inasmuch as the adjective is attributable, words like child or old man cannot constitute objects, because they are only passing states of the object, human being or animal. On the other hand with certain kinds of animals the young may differ from the fully grown through conctitutive marks, in which case a concrete noun is formed. Calf, for instance, is not expressed as young cow or young bull (*junges rind*), but by a word for an object, a noun, of its own. Over against the vast sphere of the verb, stands a small completely rigid stock of words for objects, nouns. No bridge leads from this rigid stock to the verb. There is consequently no snow to be "snowed," no "milking" of the milk; but instead the stock of concrete nouns can be supplemented by objectivizing qualities and outcomes (*Erscheinungen*), gold *e.g.* is expressed as the yellow (*hurāṣu*)
[364] the prince as the great one (*rubā'u*), but with a specific word form, serving just for qualities that are objectivized, or, the sealing makes a piece of writing a document, parallel to this in the language: objectifying of the adjective "sealed" (*kanīku* = "sealed document"). Names of professions are formed in the same way; adjectives expressing a habit are objectivized, these adjectives are nothing but attributive duratives, "murderer" *e.g.* is a quality, but butcher" (*"Schlachter"*) an object.

Considering the fact that up to this day no one has yet succeeded in ascertaining the meaning of the so-called tenses in Hebrew we can be gratified with the clear picture of Akkadian. With the revitalization of the meaning of language formation achieved falls, to be sure, again a false idea of unity, that of Semitic unity. True, there are particular features in the nature of the language that must be characterized as Semitic but things are not the way they have hitherto been presented - admittedly without much methodological reflection: only those features are part of the essential nature of Akkadian, Hebrew etc. which are at the same time Semitic. After a superficial look at the individual language every phenomenon was immediately projected unto the Semitic plane and thereby lost all colour and shape. Yet this procedure, which threw one and everything into the big Semitic pot, is still to be preferred to another one, which I would designate as the surgical one: through extensive elimination of linguistic material as mere secondary formations one fancied being able to reconstruct the original language, poor in themes and meanings, and to derive from it - as so to speak from an amorphic protoplasm containing all of them *in nuce* - all the individual languages. Were it at all possible to get to the point of reconstructing such an undifferentiated original language, it would merely be a specific application of the schematic evolutionary hypothesis, according to which we reach the so-called primitive, that is to say the coarse and undifferentiated, when we follow the creations of the human mind back to its early stage. The study of ancient civilization, however, does not confirm this hypothesis, at least, not its purely formal version, for no matter whether we deal with language, custom, law, society, or even economics, everywhere, even in the oldest available documents we encounter extraordinarily subtle differentiations and an abundance of concepts and formations.

As to the development of the Semitic languages there remains from the earlier approach the pro-
[365] blem of the origin of the closed system of conjugation. While so far it has mostly been assumed that the power of analogy, impossible to check, was vaguely responsible for the accidental spreading of meaninglessly co-existing themes, I attempt to reconstruct a prehistoric form of language by regarding as primary that root in every verbal stem, which is closest to the aspect (*Aktionsart*) inherent in the verb question, *e.g.* with "to die," or "to break" the punctual theme, with "to run" the durative theme. To this now comes, however, new problems specifically connected with the history of thought, first of all the loss of the objective aspects (*Aktionsarten*) in Hebrew and Aramaic on the one hand, the loss of the subjective aspect in Akkadian on the other. There are still remnants of the aspects (*Aktionsarten*) in all the Semitic languages: in

Hebrew, coupled with the aspect-differentiation between being and becoming; also in the difference between the stative and an *n*-prefixing inchoative with roots of the type * *šamma*, where "to be stiff" and "gradually to become stiff" are opposed to one another. There is a "historical" explanation also for the hitherto inexplicable fact of coexistence of different root classes (such as *dūm* and *damam*) with identical meaning: two different, but related classes of meaning were in use side by side. Only Hebrew[4] has retained the fluid situation which makes it possible for one and the same root to belong to two different classes of events. Once we have understood the linguistic structure we have obtained immediate access to the structure of the people's mind as well and with it one of the most important determinants of civilization, in so far as it is a creation of the mind. This important insight of WILHELM VON HUMBOLDT is the more easily applied the more alien the people in question is to us. For the Babylonian world we arrive at this picture: the constant elements which constitute the world are the few pure terms for objects. As these are so few they are understandably poor in distinguishing marks. They are not divided into classes in the way, for instance, of the African languages, in which large and small things for example represent separate classes. By contrast the numerical grouping of things is object of perception.
[366] By simple means a system of concepts of unity and plurality is created, which makes a full range of distinctions possible, thus natural pluralities (trees of a forest) and abstract ones (cities), definite and indefinite number, plurality of determined individuals (*e.g.* King A, B and C) and plurality of things exchangeable at will (five peas) etc. These differentiations are, even in Akkadian, no longer truly alive, but one common Semitic remainder is left: the sex designation of the feminine, which originally signified one out of a natural plurality, in as much as in nature a plurality of females is often correlated with one male. The object concepts are the indivisible atoms of perception. An all embracing order of classifying concepts of kind and species in unknown. Avowedly, concepts of species *are* formed, but only where practical needs require it, as where a great number of species difficult to distinguish occur, like bird, snake; but no concepts of species are formed when there are only few distinctive species like grain or metal. In this case the designation a *potiori* of the one that occurs most frequently serves, *e.g.* barley for grain.

Very general terms such as animal are also missing. Their place is taken by paraphrases, or matter stands in for species, *e.g.* wood for tree. As we have seen, beside this limited and rigid stock of substantive concepts we find a rich and multi-structured stock of states and occurrences, which are classified according to type of occurrence, whether with an eye to the occurrence itself or to its result. Yet even this classification is extant only *implicite* and does not lead to any structuring of events. The great variety of verbs does not stem from the fact that a concept was differentiated by adopting markers foreign to its nature, as *e.g.* to do something at noon time or in the evening, to eat meat or bread. They are rather tested in the practical experience of daily life and adjusted to its needs without wastage. They serve as instruments of precise observation and vivid description. Here too let us give an example: an all over concept "to take" is missing, rather, distinctions are made whether or not the "taking" leads to possession, if so whether to ownership (*leqû*) or not - *e.g.* fief, lease - (*ṣabātu*) or rather to ownership on the plane of ideas - taking of a wife, acquiring of knowledge - (*aḫāzu*); further taking without pos-
[367] session, *e.g.* involuntary taking - the wind takes a leaf away or a slave is loaded with a burden - (*wabālu*), but also voluntative, taking for transportation (*našû*): moreover whether the taking occurs in a formal act of handing over (*maḫāru*) or not; in addition there are some nuances of taking by force. These words are not connected by a common generic term "to take" nor on

4. To a limited extent this applies to the closely related Aramaic as well

the other hand can any of these meanings be further analyzed, thus there is no taking away, taking out, taking for oneself. With this we have increased the isolation of all concepts we have described by one further characteristic: the lack of relationship of the individual concepts among themselves. In a sentence, naturally, the verb is brought into a relationship with one or more objects; but this relationship does not lead to a new concept, that would enrich the world of concepts *e.g.* in the form of a compound. Accordingly: a firm connection between two atoms of language is impossible.

Every statement is objective, *i.e.* independent of the standpoint of the speaker, therefore there is no article, no difference between here and there, only to a limited extent between once and now, no moods, but minute precision in the relative sequence of what appears (*Erscheinungen*) through a rigid *consecutio temporum.* The sentence is structured analytically, it is carefully prepared by the speaker and is bound to a rigid position of words without regard for the aspect of attention. If we want to draw conclusions from this linguistic structure concerning the intellectual assets of the Babylonians, no way leads from the logical disordering of the concepts of being to theoretical knowledge. On the other hand, all becoming and having become is structured in an imaginative, graphic, vivid manner and therein lies a means for artistic formative activity. Thus, with the power to realistic reproduction, and the art of keen observation the distinctiveness of the Akkadian mind is in fact exhausted, and along with it presumably the Semitic one. In the fact, though, that the Akkadian reflects keenly and well, and also observes the sequence of occurrences lies a germ for a theoretical understanding of the phenomena of nature.

Now this language spirit (*Sprachgeist*) could never unfold independently as a civilization; there is no purely Semitic civilization in Babylonia. The civilization of that country is an amalgamation of the Semitic spirit, not, - to be sure, easily put in alien fetters - with the Sumerian, which is
[368] again characterized by a fundamentally different language form. Sumerian is extremely poor in roots; its most important function is therefore the combination of simple elements that are connected into compounds. The abstract meanings of the few ever rigid and unchanging verbal roots, are, moreover, varied through local exponents. *Isolating* Akkadian stands therefore over against *combinatory* Sumerian, a language poor in relations over against a language rich in relations. The sentence structure is peculiar. First, all things participating in the action are separated out from the totality of the concept and placed at the beginning of the sentence, then by means of the verb, they are again connected into a unit with the kinds of relationship existing between the verb and the things first in the sentence expressed by verbal prefixes. At the time when the Sumerians came into contact with the Akkadians, however, they had not *only* their language, but a supra-linguistic order of things as well, an order which itself, however, was born of the spirit of the language. This order can be imagined roughly as follows.

On the basis of the names of gods and temples we must assume that the Sumerians, even before they had writing, were a people with a rich mythology mainly explanatory in nature. But the first stage of this mythology, in which the things themselves were still gods as *e.g.* Heaven and Earth, was already long pre-historic. True, the divine heaven is still found in the later pantheon, but in a dispossessed form, it had to hand over its power to the "Mistress of Heaven," a typical instance of intellectual progress. When writing was introduced this mythological understanding of the world became a pseudo-science. By attributing a name to every thing, a name which as a sign of writing could be graphically conceived, man for the first time became aware of the difference between the world of reality and the world of thought, but that difference was then immediately cancelled out again through the identification of the two. Thus the Sumerian mind, always inclined to draw parallels, saw a well-ordered co-existence of *names* in place of the helter-skelter of *things,* and never hesitated for a moment to attribute to the names a greater measure of reality than the things.

Thus when a name like *en-ki* denoted that its bearer was the lord of the earth it was generally thought that by analyzing the names' meanings, the nature of things could be perceived. The collection and ranging of the names, which at the same time presented the order of things, was the first act of science. The name by itself, though, is not sufficient to give to things that re-
[369] lationship to other things which - as we have seen - is the main form of thought of Sumerian. For this purpose a further concept is required, that of *nam*, which is difficult to translate, roughly "the sum of effects of a thing on the outside world," which is appended to every thing in the form of a formula of fate. In addition the relationship of things among themselves is further organized by *me*, "divine order of eternal, unchangeable validity"; political affairs are organized particularly by the concepts "truth" and "right conduct" (*nig-ginna* and *nig-sisa*), *i.e.* "stable legal norm" and "social balance to be reestablished at any time by the king." This is the world of *numinous concepts of order*, numinous because the gods act upon the world through them, yet, these concepts themselves, because of the emotions attaching to them, arouse in man as they are spoken the feelings of awe due to the divine. The sum total of the acts of the divine upon the world is summed in the divine *nam* through which every god is assigned his function, while the person of the god itself is of no importance. *Nam* and *me* can pass from one god to another at will so presumably we have not monotheism, but monotheiotetism, the doctrine of *one* divinity. If only these concepts of order had lost their numinous tinge they would have become useful elements of a philosophical order of the world. On the contrary, however, the Akkadians who with enthusiasm appropriated the Sumerian concepts as well as they could, intensified, even, their religious character, for Akkadian thinking, completely opposed to the relating Sumerian one, let the Sumerian concepts of order stiffen into Semitic concepts of concrete objects. Three times the same spectacle takes place before the eyes of the observer of history. Semitic peoples, who have nothing but the realism represented by their language, seize enthusiastically upon the idea of a world order but this new active numen always remains for them a concept of a higher order, which is without influence upon the understanding of the empirical world and only becomes operative when man devotes himself to emotively emphasized religious thinking. It is an idle question to ask whether the Jewish monotheism is a higher intellectual achievement than the Babylonian concept of *one* divinity; a Babylonian scholar for whom the divinity only rules through the world order taking effect, is likely to have
[370] smiled with a superior air at the God of the Israelites always mechanically intervening just as the Jewish prophet derides the Babylonian images. The achievement of the latter consists in fetching down the concept of god from the learned sphere, so that the ordinary person can participate in it; but above all as HERMANN SCHNEIDER[5] has appropriately described it, the performance consists in their revitalizing of the divinity to ruling the makers of history from the eleatic stiffness inherent in the Sumerian concepts of order. This too, however, has its roots in the language. On the one hand we have the analytical sentences of the Akkadians always constructed in parallels, knowing only a simple sequence of events, on the other hand the most lively change in the form of sentence, aspect and focus of attention, which predestines Hebrew to history writing.

Let us briefly sketch in two spheres the spiritual fruits of the mixing of Akkadian thinking with the Sumerian civilization: science and poetry. The Akkadians were unable, just as we are, to unlock all the mysteries of the Sumerian; so, though they took over from the Sumerians the major principal religious and legal concepts, this did not lead them to systematic theoretical thinking; for they lacked the verbs required for connecting the new concepts of order. Thus all theoretical

---

5. *Kultur und Denken der Babylonier und Juden.*

science is without sentences. Its function consists in the orderly collection of things on the one hand, and, on the other, in the attribution of concepts without use of the sentence, i.e. gods are brought into a relationship with one another and with various things like stars, cultic objects, numbers, but nothing is said about the type of relationship; it remains a secret, rooted in some obscure way in that mysterious divine power, the me of the Sumerians. The form of the didactic epic too, in which the Sumerians intertwined mythology and doctrine of order as set forth above, was neither imitated nor handed on as tradition, apart from that popular concoction, the epic of the creation of the world. The only area in which the Babylonians convey wisdom in the form of statements was the practical wisdom of life. Here specifically, the eternal problem of ethics and good fortune is presented not by means of abstract theory, but through *observation* and by way of *experience* of life illustrated by parables. These latter two intellectual functions
[371] which are, as we have seen, genuinely Akkadian, have, however, erected the huge building of a science set forth in conditional sentences: the lore of omens, medicine, and law, among which the last is unfortunately least known to us, apparently because it was handed on by oral tradition.

In the same way Babylonian poetry is by nature genuinely Akkadian, as comparisons with Sumerian poetry easily show. It is true that also Sumerian knows of parallelism, but there it is used only for the sake of relational symmetry. For the Akkadian, in contrast, as for the other Semites, parallelism is, so to speak, the stereometry of the expression of thought, which is always most precisely shaped and aims for greatest expressiveness (*Pragnanz*). Any kind of rhetoric is alien to the Akkadian. The mind of the poet never rises from the real to a superior world by way of elevated speech. The work of the poet consists merely in achieving increased power of realistic description, through the simple stringing together of pictures of unsurpassable vividness. Just as the Babylonian animal relief is inimitable for all time for trueness to life, so is the picturesque in poetry, the instrument for which is the verb with its refined structure which I have tried to present above. Here too there is no trait that can be removed, no nuance that could be added, no superflous flourish, no thoughtless rhetoric. The form of poetry is based on a construction of the strophe with the most careful and regular variation of the quantity of the individual elements and of the "word-geometry," if I may be allowed to use this expression to designate artistic grouping. The metre is fully clear to us and can be derived from the language form. As speech was formed slowly, cautiously, out of ready-made concepts, each word constituted one measure of speech, only occasionally did two words constitute a double measure bound with 'legato'. The word accent was very strong, the accent of the sentence without any influence. Among the Semitic languages Ethiopic is the one most similar in this respect, but for Hebrew too we can perhaps reconstruct a stage, at which the sentence accent was unimportant, and at which each word constituted an isolated measure of speech and therefore required a certain quantity of accent and sonority. Simultaneously with the revitalizing of Hebrew through the subjective language form, presumably the accent lost its stability in the sentence, along with the appearing of the rising intonation went final stress. Every Akkadian verse ends in a trochee; the monotony thus created is balanced by
[372] carefully observed architectonics of rules of art, which are based on varying distribution of the quantitive elements of the verse and on a richly diversified arrangement of the words and sentences. This holds true of the artistic strophe, whereas popular poetry was moved from the doggerel *Knittelvers* to the "sprout" strophe, in which from very small seeds, *e.g.* from the simple trochee, longer and longer offshoots grow, up to verses of extreme length.

If even the outer form of speech proved to be partly derivable from the inner language form, that may be seen as further evidence for the importance of the latter as a synthetic unity valid for all products of the mind. For the philologist this discovery is not the purpose of investigation, but a means of investigation, which is to be preferred to every other concept of unity, by which matters of the mind are thought to cohere, as *e.g.* national character, human psychological type or the mystical unification of certain cultural dominants as cultural soul; for this concept is one immediately given, comprehensive, and it can be read simply; it is not subject to arbitrary selection. To be sure, valuable as all these concepts may be for the characterization of a people's mind, yet none of them can take the place of the immediate *perception* (*Anschauung*) of the alien life. This can only grow from the living whole, whether by philology reproducing ancient poetry, or by historical art creating anew such a whole from its parts. Yet for both the most important means of reconstruction in their attempt to grasp the structure of the alien mind is the language. Only the language discloses to the scholar the riches of the alien world of ideas; without it any kind of real understanding is impossible.

Postscript

My inaugural lecture at Leipzig, held in 1926, has programmatic character. Partly because of external factors, partly because of restrictions I had to impose upon myself I was able to return to its contents only to a minimal extent; but throughout my life I have examined these theses of mine. I regard much of what I said as basic, much requires modification, but much is viewed in a one-sided manner and is untenable. Much continued to be worked on by my pupils, especially von Soden. Other things again have been undeservedly forgotten. My age and the ever-flowing stream of current work will hardly allow me to revise it, however much I would myself like to criticize the programme I drew up forty years ago.

Chicago, 25th September 1964 Benno Landsberger

Monographic Journals of the Near East
General Editor: Giorgio Buccellati

Afroasiatic Linguistics

Volume 2
Issue 7
June 1975

Systematic vs. Autonomous Phonemics and the Hebrew Grapheme dagesh

by

Joseph L. Malone

Undena Publications Malibu 1975

AFROASIATIC LINGUISTICS

AAL includes contributions in linguistics within the vast domain of Afroasiatic (Hamito-Semitic) languages. Articles of general, theoretical interest using Afroasiatic material, descriptive, historical and comparative studies are included.

Editor: Robert Hetzron (1346 San Rafael, Santa Barbara, Ca. 93109, U.S.A.)

MONOGRAPHIC JOURNALS OF THE NEAR EAST

MJNE is a system of journals on the Near East, with each journal devoted to a specialized study area, and each issue consisting of a single article. Current journals in the system are *Afroasiatic Linguistics* and *Assur.*

General Subscription

For a prepayment of $12.50 the subscriber selects random issues from within the entire system as desired, up to a total of 200 pages. The subscriber is also entitled to (1) periodical lists of abstracts from all journals in the system, and (2) reservation to any journal within the system, whereby issues of a given journal are sent on approval immediately upon publication (and may be returned within two weeks).

Library Subscription

A prepayment of $12.50 for each journal in the system secures all issues of a single volume as soon as they are published. This subscription schedule does not allow the selection of random issues; in return, a discount is provided in the form of a greater number of pages for the basic price of $12.50 (since a volume will normally include more than 200 pages).

Library subscriptions are available to both institutions and individual scholars.

Individual issues are numbered *sequentially* within each volume. Each issue has its own pagination. A volume is closed when a total of between 200 and 250 pages is reached.

A *title page* and a *table of contents* listing all issues within each volume are sent to all subscribers at the close of a volume.

Periodicity in the order of appearance of issues is not predetermined. A volume, however, is generally completed within one year.

Institutional and Professional discount of 20% on single subscriptions (higher on larger orders). Payment must accompany orders from individuals. A handling fee of 70¢ will be charged to Libraries if order is not prepaid. Order from: UNDENA PUBLICATIONS, P.O. Box 97, Malibu, California 90265, U.S.A.
